Original title:
Tropical Temptations

Copyright © 2025 Creative Arts Management OÜ
All rights reserved.

Author: Harris Montgomery
ISBN HARDBACK: 978-1-80586-446-2
ISBN PAPERBACK: 978-1-80586-918-4

Palate of the Sun

Mango boats drift in the bay,
Giggling, the coconuts sway.
Limes chuckle with zest on the shelf,
Promising cheers with each sip of self.

Bananas in hats strut down the street,
Seashells dance with rhythm and beat.
Pineapples wear sunglasses so bright,
Laughing with the sun, what a sight!

Drifting Dreamscapes

Kiwi kites soaring so high,
Coconut clouds drift in the sky.
Papaya pirates on a smoothie spree,
Swashbuckling fruit sailing the sea.

A guava giggles at the tease,
While pineapple plays hide and seek with the breeze.
Ripe cherries bounce on jellybean waves,
In this sweet world, laughter saves.

Eden's Embrace

The candy vines twist with flair,
Fruity fairies flip in the air.
Lemons play tricks with a sly, bright grin,
While grape goblins dance and spin.

Oranges tumble, a silly sight,
Winking at the moon, so bright.
Beneath a mango tree, jokes unfold,
In this sweet paradise, life's never old.

Morning Dew on Pineapples

The dew drops tickle the vibrant crown,
As sleepy fruits slowly come down.
A watermelon yawns, stretching wide,
While a bunch of grapes giggle and slide.

Fantasies brew in each fresh squeeze,
Where nectar spills like the warmest breeze.
Sipping sunshine, a joyful toast,
To the fruity friends we love the most!

Rum-Soaked Memories

In a glass of sunshine, we sip with glee,
Every drop a giggle, just you and me.
The parrot outside joins in the cheer,
Squawking our secrets, oh dear, oh dear!

Sand between toes and laughs all around,
Our dance on the beach is joyfully sound.
With each little stumble, a smile's on the rise,
The ocean waves chuckle, beneath sunny skies.

Lush Layers of Life

In hats made of palm fronds and shirts far too bright,
We stumble through markets, oh what a sight!
With fruits stacked so high, like towers of fun,
Juggling our laughter under the sun.

The mangos keep rolling, our giggles collide,
Who knew that a fruit could make such a slide?
We're sticky and happy, can't help but to share,
A slice of sweet life, with tropical flair.

Whispering Waves

The sea tells a story as it splashes and sighs,
With fish doing backflips beneath the blue skies.
Shells whisper secrets, they tickle our toes,
While crabs in the corners perform funny shows.

Seagulls swoop low, and we start to play tag,
With each feathery dive, a laugh starts to wag.
Oh, life is a circus when waves have their say,
Just riding the tide, in our goofy ballet!

Twilight Temptations

As the sun dips low, and the stars take their stand,
We munch on sweet treats, with giggles at hand.
The evening grows silly, with fireflies aglow,
They dance in the air, putting on quite a show.

With laughter like music and playful delight,
We dance in the shadows, hearts feeling so light.
So join in the fun, let your worries just float,
In a night full of whispers, the world's a small boat.

Coconuts and Caress

In a hammock I swing, feeling quite grand,
A coconut drops, hits me on the hand.
I laugh and I grin, but oh, what a pain,
This tropical fruit dance drives me insane!

The palm trees lean in, tossing their leaves,
While seagulls around me plot and deceive.
A crab scuttles by, he's showing off flair,
As I sip on my drink without a care!

Tropical Escapade

I stepped on a shell, what a squeaky surprise,
The locals all giggle, they give me the eyes.
With a splash and a dash, I trip in the tide,
Flipping like fish, oh where shall I hide?

The sun starts to set, painting skies with blush,
A monkey above laughs with a cheeky hush.
He steals my last chip, and I'm left with a grin,
Who knew a beach day could be such a win?

Sunlit Desires

Bikini too tight, oh what a tight squeeze,
I try to relax, but I'm stuck like a breeze.
The sun's baking down, my drink's gone awry,
Just as I sip, a wave splashes by!

The sand's in my toes, it tickles and rolls,
I dance like a crab, with laughter and trolls.
A toucan flies by, gives me a smirk,
Taunting my fumbles, oh what a perk!

Sands of Allure

The beach ball rolls off, oh where has it fled?
Chasing it down, I tumble ahead.
I faceplant in sand, looking like a mess,
Even the gulls can't resist, I confess!

With towels all tangled, we laugh 'til we cry,
The sun's blazing down, but we won't say goodbye.
A sip of cold punch, now it's all a blur,
Who knew the beach could cause such a stir?

Sun-Dappled Whimsy

The coconut fell with a splat,
A monkey laughed, what a chat!
With lime in his drink and a hat,
He danced like a silly acrobat.

The sunbeams played on the sand,
A crab made a castle so grand.
Sharing secrets, the seashells had planned,
As waves clapped their happy, wet hands.

A parrot squawked jokes in a tree,
While tourists burst out with glee.
Laughter echoed from sea to sea,
In this sunny land, wild and free.

So come barefoot and join the fun,
Grab a drink, let the joy run.
With giggles aplenty, and puns spun,
Under the grin of the big hot sun.

Cascade of Joy

A waterfall splashed all around,
Where fish wore hats, quite profound.
They swam in pairs, spun round and round,
While frogs croaked tunes, a sweet sound.

The umbrellas danced with the breeze,
Swaying back like a teasing tease.
With juice in hand, it's sure to please,
As laughter bubbles like sodas, with ease.

A sunburnt tourist slipped in the mud,
Landed right with a big ol' thud!
But even that couldn't spoil the flood,
Of joy that rolled in like a warm cuddle.

So let's all splash in this bliss,
Where every fumble is hit or miss.
With smiles exchanged and a wet kiss,
Adventure awaits in the joy we can't dismiss.

Passionate Paradise

A pineapple wore a polka dot dress,
While mangoes giggled, oh what a mess!
Dancing with rhythm, so bold, no less,
They twirled by the shore in sheer happiness.

The sun wore shades, looking quite cool,
While jellyfish bobbed like a soft jewel.
With seagulls calling, like a wise old school,
It felt like laughter was the main rule.

The sand was a couch for the lazy souls,
Bikes zoomed past with raucous roles.
Each wave that crashed was laughter's tolls,
In this paradise where joy consoles.

Let's raise a toast to the fruity scene,
With all our friends, and a spirit keen.
In this land where joy reigns supreme,
Every moment sparkles like a dream.

Harmonies in Bloom

The flowers giggled, dressed in hues,
With bees that danced to their sweet blues.
They bumbled by, spreading joyful news,
Every petal flicked a cheeky muse.

A turtle tried to hula with grace,
While flamingos struck a silly pose face.
The sunflowers turned to cheer this race,
While rainbows winked in a vibrant embrace.

The picnic spread was a funny sight,
With ants debating what cake was right.
Laughter echoed in the morning light,
Where even the breeze took flight, delight.

So come join this garden of laughter,
Where fun grows wild and the joy is after.
In this, the best of nature's chapter,
Every moment blooms with cheerful rapture.

Swaying Palms

Undervertigo, palms sway and dance,
Wearing coconuts like hats in a trance.
The lizards are gossiping, oh what a show,
While the sun laughs at the wind's silly blow.

Bouncing beach balls on parade, oh what fun,
Seagulls join in, thinking they're the one.
Flip-flops chatter like gossiping friends,
As waves roll in, all worries just mend.

Blissful Horizons

In flip-flop fashion, we strut and prance,
Chasing crabs down the shore, what a chance!
With ice creams melting, drips like our care,
We laugh 'til we tumble, sand in our hair.

Beach umbrellas dance, colors collide,
While sunburns battle each seaside stride.
A seagull steals fries, a daring heist,
We cheer for the bandit—oh, what a feast!

Coral-Blue Reverie

Diving in bubbles, we giggle and glide,
With snorkels and flippers, we swagger with pride.
Fish wear sunglasses, swimming with flair,
While starfish take selfies without a care.

Under the surface, a disco awaits,
Where dolphins dance, time just dilates.
A treasure of laughter, we dig in the sand,
With shells as our jewels, oh isn't life grand?

Bounty of the Isles

From mango to guava, the feast is on call,
Each fruit tells a tale, oh taste them all!
Banana splits winking with cherry on top,
Let's create a ruckus, don't ever stop!

Laughter ricochets like the waves on the shore,
This island of joy, who could ask for more?
In hammock debates, who shall sway the best?
Sipping sweet punches, we're truly blessed!

Emerald Oasis

In the shade of a palm,
A monkey stole my drink,
With laughter in the breeze,
I couldn't help but wink.

Coconuts roll and drop,
As I dodge a flying hat,
The sun laughs in the sky,
Oh, the things I have sat!

A toucan on a branch,
Mocks my sunburned nose,
While lizards in sunglasses,
Strike poses in rows.

In this green paradise,
Life's a comic spree,
With hiccups and giggles,
Nature's jester's glee.

Paradise in Bloom

A flower said 'Hello!'
To a bee buzzing by,
He replied with a dance,
And they both reached for the sky.

Pineapple on my head,
A crown fit for a king,
But the wind stole my fruit,
Oh, what a funny fling!

Bananas on the beach,
Rolling with the tide,
They slip and slide around,
In a fruity joyride.

Every bloom laughs out loud,
Each petal has a quirk,
In this patch of vibrant fun,
Where giggles are the work.

Enchanted Shores

Waves crash with a giggle,
As sand plays peek-a-boo,
A crab wearing a hat,
Dances just for you.

Seagulls try their best,
To snatch away my snack,
But I toss them some chips,
While they eye my backpack.

A dolphin leaps so high,
With flips to make hearts skip,
Yet falters on the wave,
And takes a salty dip.

Here on shores of laughter,
Magic weaves through sand,
Every moment sparkles bright,
As life takes us by hand.

Exotic Dreams

In a hammock, I sway,
As lizards sing a tune,
Their chorus makes me snort,
And dance beneath the moon.

Fruit bats overhead,
Holding nightly raves,
While I trip over roots,
Trying not to misbehave.

Parrots squawk like comedians,
Telling jokes on the fly,
While I laugh till I cry,
And wave the night goodbye.

In this land of whimsy,
Where smiles bloom for days,
Life's a carnival ride,
In the funniest of ways.

Vibrant Fronds

Underneath the swaying trees,
Lizards dance with such great ease.
Palm fronds whisper silly tales,
Of coconut halves and seagull trails.

Flip-flops flapping, laughter loud,
Sipping drinks, we feel so proud.
A crab in a tutu, what a sight,
Shimmies sideways, steals the night.

Mango mishaps on our shirts,
Sticky fingers, slightly hurt.
But oh, those smiles can't be beat,
Every moment feels so sweet.

A parrot squawks from high above,
It claims the best sunbathing spot with love.
While we watch and share a chuckle,
In this paradise, none dare to buckle.

Oceanside Promises

Waves are crashing, surfboards fly,
Seagulls swoop and cheekily cry.
In the sand, a lost shoe lies,
But who cares? We're on the rise!

Sandcastles wobble, dreams collide,
With popsicle sticks as our proud guide.
A beach ball bounces, slips, then lands,
On someone's picnic, now it's in their hands!

Crabs wearing sunglasses, looking so cool,
They strut by the water, breaking every rule.
We giggle as they scurry away,
Ruined our picnic? What can we say!

A tightrope walk on the shoreline's edge,
Hope we don't slip, oh, what a pledge!
But laughter rides the salty breeze,
As we chase our pals among the trees.

Kaleidoscope of Colors

Painted skies and berry pies,
The ocean's hue, a dazzling rise.
Neon fish in swirling spree,
Invite us to join their jubilee!

Mango moons and guava stars,
Taste of summer from afar.
Sunshine spills from coconut husks,
While laughter blends with rhythmic gusts.

Oranges giggle, lime's a tease,
Every fruit nods in summer's breeze.
With a splash! A pineapple dive,
Who knew juice could feel so alive?

Kites in colors, dancing high,
Onlookers cheer—oh me, oh my!
Chasing dreams like we're all kids,
In a world where color never bids.

The Sweetness of Life

A cookie crumb on a sun-kissed nose,
Life is sweet, just like it goes.
With chocolate waves and whipped cream clouds,
We skip around in vibrant crowds.

Pineapple pizza? That's a thrill,
We won't judge, just get your fill.
Chasing ice cream on a hot day,
Melting drips? Hip hip hooray!

Hiccups from laughter, so absurd,
A dance-off? You've heard the word!
Belly flops by the little ones,
Joyful splashes, purest fun!

So raise a toast with fizzy drinks,
Join the giggles, share the winks.
In this life, we twirl and glide,
Finding sweetness in each ride.

The Fruitful Breeze

Coconut fell with a thud,
The monkeys laughed in the mud.
Mangoes dipped in the sea,
Sending splashes, oh so free.

Passion fruit danced on a line,
Sipping juice, feeling divine.
Pineapples wore their best hats,
Chasing crabs, oh silly chats.

Bananas slipped in a race,
While papayas played with grace.
Limes tossed laughter all around,
In this feast, joy was found.

Sunshine bubbles in the air,
Amidst the fruits, we have our share.
With giggles, let the day tease,
As we float on this fruit-laden breeze.

Island Reverie

A parrot squawked a silly tune,
As coconuts fell, they bounced like a balloon.
Sandy toes and sun-kissed hair,
Our laughter echoed everywhere.

The hammock swung, a cozy ride,
While seashells played, they took our side.
Flip-flops danced in wobbly glee,
As waves sang songs of jubilee.

Crabs did the cha-cha on the shore,
While jellyfish flashed, we cried for more.
A turtle checked its watch and smiled,
Who knew beach life could be so wild?

Island dreams float in the sky,
With each giggle, time just flies by.
As seagulls join in the fun parade,
In this reverie, worries all fade.

Dances in the Sand

Sandcastles stronger than they seem,
Waves crash down on our sandy dream.
Children's giggles paint the air,
As seagulls swoop with flair to spare.

Shells collected for a beach parade,
Each one unique, a treasure made.
Crabs in tutus twirl and spin,
As beach balls bounce, let the fun begin.

Winds whisper secrets of the tide,
Where laughter bubbles, there's no need to hide.
With each splash and skip in the surf,
Get ready now for some sandy turf!

The sun dips low, a golden hue,
As the party winds down, we bid adieu.
Yet in our hearts, the dances stay,
A silly tune that won't fade away.

Hibiscus Hues

Hibiscus blooms in shades of cheer,
Dancing petals draw us near.
Under the sun, a bright bouquet,
Colorful frolics light the day.

With sunglasses perched, we strike a pose,
As sunflowers giggle, their laughter grows.
Palm fronds flap like dancing fans,
In this garden, joy expands.

As butterflies flit, they wink and tease,
While bees hum by, buzzing with ease.
A playful breeze whirls all around,
In the floral realm, fun is found.

At sunset, hues melt into joy,
As the colors mix—oh, what a ploy!
Let's paint our lives in vibrant view,
In laughter and petals, we'll find our cue.

Emerald Embrace

In a land where coconuts sway,
Monkeys dance the night away.
Pineapple hats on heads so bright,
Crabs play maracas under the light.

The ocean teases with a splash,
Surfboards zoom, they make a crash.
Flipping fish with sunny grins,
While sandcastles sprout tiny twin sins.

Cocktails swirl with vibrant hues,
Parrots gossip the latest news.
Seashells laugh as waves retreat,
With goofy hermits dancing on their feet.

Gather 'round for the limbo game,
Giggling under the moon's soft flame.
In this paradise, nothing's a bore,
Join the fun, there's always more!

Flavors of Sun and Sea

Mango sorbet melts with glee,
As coconuts grin, bright and free.
Skimpy shorts and sunburned toes,
The scent of grilled fish, oh how it glows!

Flip-flops squeak on sandy paths,
As laughter echoes, it's pure math.
A seagull snatches a snack in flight,
While friends chase each other, what a sight!

Oysters wear pearls, so fancy dressed,
While sloths delegate rest with zest.
Smoothies dance in vibrant blends,
Hawaiian shirts—on you depends!

Join the barbecue, bring the fun,
Belly laughs under the blazing sun.
Chasing crabs, it's a hilarious spree,
In every bite, taste the jubilee!

Lullabies of the Lagoon

In the lagoon where the frogs croon,
Crickets play their favorite tune.
Alligators chill with hats so grand,
While fish trade gossip, oh so planned.

Starry nights, a glowing track,
See the fireflies dance, don't look back.
Turtles race on an evening stroll,
While dragonflies serve up thoughts we stole.

Wet socks trailing in the mist,
A mermaid giggles—you might've missed.
Water lilies wear crowns of dew,
Whispered secrets shared between the two.

The moon's a witness to our pranks,
As we build boats from love and flanks.
In this haven, we laugh with ease,
Swaying gently with a tropical breeze!

Cinnamon Starlight

Under a sky with stars so bright,
Cinnamon rolls in a sugar fight.
A parrot steals my last sweet bite,
What a cheeky move—oh, what a sight!

Fire pits crackle with twinkling flames,
S'mores and giggles, we play the games.
While iguanas pose in stylish hats,
The sand is a canvas for playful chats.

Sunsets splash colors, bold and wide,
As we share tales of our wacky ride.
Surfboards whirling, laughter surges,
In this carnival, joy emerges.

Chasing shadows till the night,
Cocktail umbrellas, oh what a sight!
With laughter as our guiding light,
We dance beneath the cinnamon starlight!

Flora's Embrace

In a garden so lush and bright,
Where flowers dance in the soft moonlight,
The petals giggle, the leaves do sway,
They whisper secrets of a sunny day.

A bee in a tux, looking quite dapper,
Buzzes around like a flamboyant rapper.
With pollen pockets full of zest,
He tells the blooms they're truly blessed.

A parrot perched with a joke to share,
Contemplates life in the fragrant air.
With feathers bright, he plays a tune,
That lifts your spirits beneath the moon.

In this embrace of petals and cheer,
Nature laughs, 'Come join us here!'
So let's frolic amongst the vines,
And sip nectar sourced from flower wines.

Coral Cauldron

In a sea of colors, lo and behold,
Coral reefs sit, like treasures of gold.
Fish in tuxedos, swimming with flair,
They throw a party, there's fun in the air.

An octopus chef stirs a bubbling stew,
With spices so wild and flavors so new.
He twirls his arms while the crabs clink glasses,
To toast the joys that undersea life passes.

A turtle in shades, so cool and profound,
Claims he knows where the best laughs are found.
With jokes that ripple like waves on the shore,
He says, "Join the fun! There's so much in store!"

In this cauldron of life, the laughter runs deep,
Where coral and critters make promises to keep.
So dive right in, let your worries flee,
And dance with the tide of this wacky sea.

The Orchid's Kiss

In the jungle's heart, orchids adorn,
Petals that flutter, a sight to be sworn.
They pose in glam, with a wink and a twist,
Inviting you in for a floral tryst.

A monkey swings by, adorned with vines,
He grins and teases, "Let's sip some wines!"
With laughter erupting from branches up high,
He says, "You can't leave till you give it a try!"

Sweet scents fill the air, tickling the nose,
While the orchids whisper, "Be brave, who knows?"
A dance of the blossoms, a riot of hues,
Each kiss from a petal spurs laughter and views.

So frolic through blooms, let joy be your guide,
In the midst of flowers, take life for a ride.
Embrace the absurd, let giggles take flight,
In the orchid's kiss, all is pure delight.

Temptation by the Sea

On a sun-drenched beach, where the sand is gold,
Waves frolic forth with a laughter untold.
Seagulls pull pranks, stealing fries from your plate,
While crabs in their shells plot an escape fate.

A beach ball bounces, full of hot air,
As children giggle in the salty, warm glare.
The sun soars high, casting playful rays,
While ice cream drips down in a summer blaze.

Shells hidden treasures, with stories to tell,
Whispering secrets of the ocean's swell.
A dolphin pops up with a splash and a grin,
Inviting you over to the dolphin swim.

So let's dance on the shore with flip-flops unstrung,
With laughter and joy, let our hearts be young.
For by the sea's charm, we shall forever stay,
In a whirl of fun, come join the ballet!

Cascades of Color

Sun hats waving in the breeze,
Mangoes roll like pesky bees.
Flip-flops dance on golden sand,
While coconut drinks in hand stand.

Pineapples wear silly grins,
Hula hoops spun by clumsy sins.
Brightly colored fish take a dive,
As laughter bubbles, we come alive.

Bikinis clash in wild array,
As seagulls steal our chips away.
A parrot squawks a cheeky tune,
Near sun-soaked shores, we croon and swoon.

In this candy-colored land,
Joy and giggles go hand in hand.
So let the colors shine so bold,
As we create stories to be told.

Azure Embrace

In the shade of azure skies,
Sipping drinks while sand flies,
Giggling crabs with funny shells,
Share secrets where the ocean dwells.

Palm trees dance, a wobbly show,
As we twist in a limbo slow.
A sudden splash, a cannonball,
Then funny faces as we fall.

The beach ball's lost, it's gone astray,
Chasing it turns into play.
Splashing water, slippery feet,
Our sandy antics can't be beat.

Sunset paints the sky so bright,
With cotton candy, what a sight!
We laugh, we cheer, and shout hooray,
For joy in blue will always stay.

Coconut Grove Chronicles

In a grove where coconuts sway,
We play games in a silly way.
Sipping milk from grassy shells,
With giggles loud, oh how it swells!

Mud pies splatter, laughter roars,
As we build our sandy shores.
Bamboo sticks for swords we wield,
Champions of this sunny field.

A rogue raccoon joins the fray,
Steals our snacks, oh what a day!
Chasing him, we trip and fall,
Face first into a coconut ball.

Underneath the twinkling stars,
We swap tales of our silly wars.
For memories made in this land,
Brought forth by laughter, hand in hand.

A Symphony of Flavor

Pineapple pizza, such delight,
Makes taste buds dance through the night.
Mango mojitos, a playful spritz,
Coconut cake, oh how it fits!

Grapefruit giggles on a stick,
As flavors fuse in a fruity trick.
Chilies spice up our goofy grin,
While fruity bites make us spin.

Chocolate dipped bananas run fast,
In this feast, we forget the past.
Waffle cones with sea salt dreams,
Our laughter blends with the sun's beams.

So bring on the tastes, wild and bold,
In a carnival of flavor to behold.
We chuckle and munch with carefree glee,
As this magical feast sets us free.

Island Heartbeat

Palm trees sway with a silly dance,
Coconuts laugh as they take a chance.
A parrot squawks jokes from high above,
As I sip fruit punch with a twist of love.

Sunbathers roll like hot dogs on the sand,
A beach ball flies, but oh, what a hand!
Flip-flops flapping like a marching band,
Shells are auditioning—who's got the strand?

Crabs in tuxedos strut on by,
While a sea turtle decides to try.
Dancing on waves, with the sun in sight,
We giggle at fish doing karaoke all night.

Like a conga line, this island groove,
With laughter bubbling, it sets the move.
In the hammock, dreams can expand,
As breezes tickle, our hearts are fanned.

Secret Coves

Whispers float through the jade-blue sea,
In hidden nooks, where mermaids flee.
Flipping flounders and seahorses prance,
While octopuses plot their shimmery dance.

A lighthouse winks, quite up to no good,
It's plotting a party, oh yes, it would!
A treasure map led us here quite clear,
But all we found was a raucous cheer.

With mangoes and laughter, we share a feast,
Jellyfish juggle like a funky beast.
Squid in sunglasses, oh what a sight,
As we dive into the frothy delight.

The waves chuckle, tickling our toes,
As we race the tide, where no one knows.
In these secret nooks, so snug and bright,
Life's a carnival under the moonlight.

Sunset's Caress

As the sun dips low, a colorful show,
Sky paints a canvas with a cheeky glow.
Tiki torches giggle in the evening breeze,
While flip-flops shuffle as we join the tease.

Sipping on cocktails that twirl and swirl,
Umbrellas dancing as our worries whirl.
Sandy toes wiggling to the crickets' tune,
Where laughter blooms beneath the lazy moon.

A huarache hat held high, makes me grin,
As we capture moments with a silly spin.
Salsa on the shore, a feast for the soul,
This sunset's magic makes everyone whole.

With goofy grins, we watch the stars peep,
As memories weave and laughter takes leap.
In the sweet embrace of the twilight's kiss,
Each moment's a treasure, we simply can't miss.

Serpentine Shorelines

Waves twist and turn like a playful snake,
With salty giggles that make us quake.
Sunburns smiling, a comical sight,
As we frolic and tumble, oh what a night!

Seagulls gossip, squawking with flair,
While surfers ride waves with wind-tousled hair.
Each splash a chuckle, each crash a cheer,
At our serpentine beach, there's nothing to fear.

A conch shell horn blares, start the dance,
As crabs join in for a crumpet prance.
Lemonade spills and laughter flies,
Under the watchful and twinkling skies.

Building sandcastles, we cheer and boast,
While sand gets stuck and we giggle the most.
With every tide pooling stories and play,
At the serpentine shores, we'll forever sway.

Tidal Journeys

Waves crash, a slippery race,
Seagulls steal my lunch with grace.
I dive for fries, they dive for crisps,
Sunburned back, we're all in this.

Sandy toes and squawking cheer,
Lifeguard's whistle, loud and clear.
Bucket hat's my sunblock shield,
Running from waves, I just may yield.

Tide comes in, my laughter swells,
Collecting shells, and some fish smells.
Taking selfies, goofy grins,
Sandcastles with candy limbs.

Seashells whisper, tales they weave,
Vacation's joy, I can't believe.
Ancient crabs hold court with flair,
Funny friends are everywhere.

Sweet Nectar of Nature

Buzzing bees, they dance and hum,
In search of juice, they come undone.
Flower crowns made of petals bright,
Sipping nectar, what a sight!

Juicy mango, drips on my chin,
Tropical punch makes me spin.
Worms in the ground, they do a jig,
Plants all around, they live big!

Fruits fall down, plop, what a mess,
I slip and slide, in my sundress.
Coconuts land with a thud,
Refreshing drinks or sticky mud?

Nature's a riot, laughter erupts,
Squirrels sing while the cactus interrupts.
Bees wear tuxedos, oh so neat,
Each bloom a banquet, what a treat!

A Dance with Breeze

Palm trees sway, a groovy twist,
Breezy whispers, I can't resist.
Flip-flops flop, but I don't care,
Dancing silly, right in the air.

Air so thick, it tickles my nose,
Wind blows strong, it teases my toes.
Coconut hats bounce round my head,
A conga line, let's dance instead!

Dolphins laugh as they swim by,
Skipping stones, I aim for the sky.
Sunset glow on my golden skin,
With every giggle, let the fun begin.

Seagulls join with a caw and glide,
Ocean's rhythm, a joyful ride.
Breezes carrying laughter and cheer,
Every moment, my heart's full here.

Luminous Flora

Glow of flowers in the night,
Dancing under the moonlight bright.
Fragrant breezes tickle my nose,
Laughter blooms as chaos grows.

Glow worms wiggle in the grass,
Each one shines, a tiny class.
Flamboyant petals wave and cheer,
Nature's show, it's premiere here!

Lightbulb plants with vibrant hues,
A funny sight, a plant that wooze.
Wiggly vines, I trip and fall,
Nature's humor, catering all.

Chasing fireflies, oh what fun,
Playing tag 'til the day is done.
Luminous flora, my friends agree,
In this wild garden, we're the spree!

Beachside Reveries

Sandcastles rise with a wink,
Seagulls steal fries in a blink.
Sunscreen smears on my nose,
Life's a laugh, in beachy clothes.

Fruits on the grill, a burst of cheer,
Watermelons giggle, they know no fear.
Flip-flops dance on the warm, soft ground,
Joyful laughter is the sweetest sound.

Crabs in a race, they scuttle with glee,
Who knew they could be so sprightly and free?
A beach ball bounces, it flies in the air,
Land it on someone's head if you dare!

As the sun dips low, we toast with delight,
To sandy adventures that last through the night.
With friends all around, we're rich and we're bold,
These beachside moments are treasures untold.

Lush Labyrinths

In gardens so green, we dance round the bends,
With vines that tickle and laughter that blends.
Bees are our gossip, they buzz and conspire,
Through leaves where the sun and the mischief conspire.

Bananas wear hats, it's a silly parade,
Pineapples giggle, they're never afraid.
With coconuts laughing, we swing like the breeze,
In jungles of joy, we do as we please.

Papayas are pondering, ripe with delight,
While mangoes trade jokes, both ripe and polite.
Slug races commence, the slowest of thrills,
We cheer for the underdog, fueled by our spills.

Through lush labyrinths, we crisscross and play,
With smiles and sunshine, we brighten the way.
Every twist and turn, a new joke awaits,
In this vibrant green maze, life's laughter creates.

The Melodies of Mangoes

Mangoes a-jive in the afternoon sun,
With juicy refrains, they dance just for fun.
Peeling their laughter, sweet nectar flows,
A symphony of flavor only summer knows.

On fruity stages, they leap and they bound,
In orchards of joy, their laughter is found.
Swaying in rhythm, they croon with delight,
Their chorus of sweetness, a pure summer night.

Chop-chop the beats, let the salsa commence,
Mangoes in motion, a fruity romance.
With passion-filled bites, we sway side to side,
In the dance of the season, we take the wild ride.

As night wraps us up in a warm, cozy glow,
We toast to the mangoes, the stars in a row.
These melodies linger, like whispers of bliss,
In each juicy bite, there's a tune we won't miss.

Enigma of the Islands

Islands that chuckle, with waves full of glee,
Tropical riddles, like a puzzle to see.
With footprints in sand that tell tales so sly,
Each sunset's a secret, a wink from the sky.

Kites that soar high, like our spirits afloat,
A llama in shades, wearing sunstitched coat.
Mystic coconuts whisper in jest,
As they juggle the pearls that the ocean had blessed.

Dancing to rhythms the breeze likes to share,
The fish make a splash, as if they're aware.
Laughter aplenty, with seashells that sing,
The enigma of islands, oh, what joy they bring!

With evenings of warmth, beneath starry skies,
These mysteries linger, like laughter and sighs.
In this whimsical land, we joyfully roam,
Where every tide beckons us back to our home.

Fruitful Paradise

In a land where fruits just smile,
Mangoes dance and pineapples beguile.
Coconuts play hide and seek,
While papayas giggle, cheek to cheek.

Beneath the palm, a party's set,
Bananas peel, and no one's upset.
Oranges juggle, oh what a sight,
Making fruit salads feel just right.

Kiwi birds in shoes of flair,
Strut their stuff without a care.
Berries wear hats of vivid hues,
How could one ever refuse?

In this realm of fruity cheer,
Laughter echoes, loud and clear.
Grab a slice, take a bite,
In this paradise, all feels right.

The Lure of Lush

Lush green leaves wave a big hello,
As beach balls bounce and flip to and fro.
Coconuts roll with giddy delight,
Making their moves as day turns night.

Limes and mangoes play a prank,
While guavas gather in a tank.
Then each fruit takes a silly stance,
Grapes begin their wobble dance.

Under the sun, oh what a scheme,
Watermelons spill their juicy dream.
Kites fly high, the colors clash,
As laughter and juice come out in a splash.

So come and join this fruity fun,
Where each day feels like a run.
Grab a cocktail, let's unwind,
In this lush land, joy's enshrined.

Robins' Coastal Song

Robins sing in colorful charm,
While crabs perform their silly harm.
Seagulls preen, their feathers bright,
Chasing waves, what a funny sight.

Fish join in, they splash around,
Dancing beneath where joy is found.
Starfish laugh on sandy shore,
While seaweed wobbles, wanting more.

A beach ball bounces with a smirk,
As shells gossip, oh what a quirk!
Sandy toes tap a catchy tune,
Under the warmth of a laughing moon.

With each wave comes a friendly tease,
Nature's humor brings us ease.
Sing along, it's quite a fling,
In the coastal song, let joy ring!

The Call of the Tropics

In the tropics where humor's bright,
Pineapples giggle with delight.
Cherries burst with playful cheer,
While surfboards glide without a fear.

Frogs wear hats, quite out of date,
As they leap around and celebrate.
Bikinis on trees in a sunny spree,
Nature takes on a quirky glee.

Here the sun beams with a wink,
Mermaids chat over a drink.
Lizards strut in shades of green,
Making the forest a lively scene.

With a grin, the breeze does tease,
Whispering secrets through the leaves.
Join the laughter, take a stroll,
In the tropics, let's feel whole!

Velvet Skies and Ocean Blues

Under velvet skies, we chase the breeze,
With jellybeans dancing on the palm trees.
A crab in a tux, so dapper and neat,
Takes a sidestep groove with two left feet.

Coconuts chuckle, they wobble and sway,
As the sun wears shorts on a bright sunny day.
Fish in the pool play a game of charades,
While seagulls squawk out their best serenades.

Tanned toes in sand, what a clammy delight,
A sunburned nose that glows red by night.
Beware of that drink with a colorful straw,
It wiggles and giggles; oh, what a flaw!

When twilight arrives, we find a new dance,
To the rhythm of waves that invite us to prance.
With laughter echoing 'neath stars like confetti,
Who knew paradise could be this confetti?

Ferns and Fantasies

In lush green jungles, the whispers are loud,
Frogs in tuxedos take pride in their crowd.
Parrots are gossiping over ripe mangoes,
While the iguanas strike silly poses and show.

With ferns as our fans, we lounge in the shade,
Giggling at snails in their slow-moving parade.
A monkey named Fred swings with such grace,
But trips on a vine and lands on his face!

Bananas a-swinging, they tease our delight,
"Catch us if you can!" they chirp, quite polite.
We chase after dreams as the butterflies grin,
And dance with the shadows where laughter begins.

Oh, the wild adventures this wilderness brings,
Like hula-hooping with imaginary rings.
Let's twirl and skip 'neath the smiling sun's beams,
In the land made of magic and whimsical dreams!

A Song of Solstice

With a toucan's song playing high in the trees,
We sashay through the market, indulging with ease.
Pineapple pizzas? What a curious quest!
But every bite taken, it scores a sweet jest!

Sun-kissed cabanas, all painted so bright,
A hammock's embrace keeps us up through the night.
The sun winks at us with a cheeky delight,
While fireflies dance in a sparkly flight.

Lemonade rivers flow smoothly like dreams,
As we float on donuts and swim in whipped creams.
A game of piñata with fruits dangling low,
Each swing brings laughter and a sugary glow.

So raise up your glass to this jolly good cheer,
Celebrate seasons with sunshine and beer.
In this land full of giggles and mirth we shall stay,
Where every day feels like a festival play!

Whispers Among the Tides

Under the moon's gaze, the tide spills its tales,
A dolphin named Gary wears fancy brails.
He juggles sea stars as waves gently chat,
While crabs form a conga, all dressed like a brat.

The seaweed sways like it knows all the fun,
Teaching octopuses how to run.
Flip-flops are flapping on feet that are spry,
As the night sparkles bright with a starry-sky-high.

Anemones giggle as fish swim on by,
Spinning 'round shells, giving friendship a try.
The tide's gentle whispers are filled with delight,
Creating a chorus that lasts through the night.

So here's to the waves and the secrets they hold,
To the laughter and joy in the stories retold.
In this oceanic haven where silliness thrives,
We dance to the rhythm of joyful, bright lives!

Lullabies of the Lagoon

In the lagoon where the frogs croon,
Fish wear hats made from a palm leaf spoon.
Lemurs swing in the trees so high,
Singing lullabies to the moon in the sky.

A crab in a tux makes a fancy parade,
While turtles get lost in a crumply charade.
The waves giggle, tickling the shore,
As sandcastles brace for a salty encore.

A flotilla of ducks in a conga line,
Chasing the sun, oh isn't it fine?
A dolphin does flips, a clownfish protests,
In this lagoon, life's a wild fest!

So close your eyes, let the laughter sway,
For the lagoon sings a silly ballet!
With each gentle wave, a chuckle will bloom,
In the heart of the night, feel the fun resume.

Fragrant Breezes

A breeze comes in with a giggly scent,
Pineapples dance like they pay no rent.
The coconuts chuckle, hanging so free,
While flowers gossip in colors, you'll see.

A parrot sidesteps with flamboyant flair,
Joking with iguanas that lounge in the air.
Mangoes spill secrets on the sunlit path,
Causing all creatures to burst into laugh!

Bananas wear sunglasses, sunbathing bright,
As guavas throw parties from morning till night.
The air hums tunes of the funniest kind,
In the fragrant breeze, joy's what you find!

So dance with the flavors, let the giggles flow,
In a world painted sweet, where joys overflow.
With every soft sigh, let your cares tease and flee,
In the fragrant breezes, how funny life can be!

Mango Moonlight

Under the mango, the moon gives a wink,
As critters gather for a silly drink.
A party of shadows with hats made of leaves,
Where the humor is rich and the laughter just cleaves.

The mangoes are ripe, glowing golden and bright,
Spinning tales of mischief in the soft moonlight.
Lizards joke about who wears the best skin,
While the mango's sweet juice drips off their chin.

Crickets play poker while frogs hum a tune,
As turtles try juggling with an old fish balloon.
Under the stars, a fun frolic begins,
In this mango-lit night, everybody grins.

So let's dance through the grass, till the night is all done,
With mango moonlight and laughter so fun!
Close your eyes, feel the joy as it glows,
In this playful night where the silliness flows!

Dance of the Hibiscus

In the garden, where hibiscus sway,
They sport little skirts for a lively ballet.
With each gentle breeze, they twirl and they spin,
Teaching the daisies how to join in.

Bees wear tiny shoes as they buzz all around,
Joining the beat in this giggly playground.
A dandy old snail brings his best ukulele,
Crooning sweet songs that turn every head really.

Sunsets giggle as colors explode,
While chubby-cheeked puppies race down the road.
All join the dance, laughter ringing so clear,
In the ballet of blooms, silliness here!

So sway with the petals, embrace every chime,
In this dance of the hibiscus, feel the rhythm of rhyme.
With smiles and joy, let your spirits ascend,
In a garden of laughter, where fun has no end!

Breeze of Serendipity

On a sunny day, I lost my hat,
Chased by a parrot who thought it was fat.
I tripped on a coconut, let out a squeal,
While sipping my juice—oh, what a meal!

A crab stole my sandwich, danced on the shore,
He wiggled his claws like a showbiz chore.
I laughed at the antics of all the beach pals,
While jellyfish wobbled like goofy gals.

In the warm sun, I see quite the sight,
A dolphin does backflips, oh what delight!
I tried to join in but fell on my face,
Now the fish are the ones who are winning this race!

With each wave that breaks, laughter fills the air,
Life's a wild ride without a single care.
So join in the fun, yes, don't be a bore,
Let's dance with the sea, and maybe explore!

Paradise Whispers

In a hammock, I snooze and sway,
Dreams of coconuts come out to play.
I hear the crabs tell jokes so sly,
While the coconut tree waves goodbye.

With sunburnt noses and silly dance,
We trip on sand and lose our chance.
The piña coladas spill on the floor,
Laughter erupts, who could ask for more?

Flip-flops fly and sunscreen splats,
Sticky fingers on tropical chats.
The monkeys giggle in the lush green,
As we chase them down like we're on screen.

So come enjoy the island cheer,
Bring your weird self; we hold you dear.
We'll laugh and sing, the world's our stage,
In this paradise, we turn the page.

Sunlit Serenade

Beneath the sun, we play all day,
Float like a beach ball, life's a buffet.
Sandy toes and wobbly chairs,
Seagulls squawk with loads of shares.

Juicy fruits make our faces shine,
We slip on watermelons, oh so fine!
The rhythm of waves matches our beat,
We dance on shells, now that's a treat!

With sun hats askew, drinks in hand,
We attempt to surf on the soft, warm sand.
But oops! We land with a splashy thud,
Making everyone roar, 'Oh, that's a dud!'

Under a sky so brilliantly blue,
We embrace the moments, just me and you.
With every giggle and ticklish wave,
Life's a mirage, fun and brave!

Lush Secrets of the Isles

In a jungle thick with fruits galore,
We munch on papayas, can't ask for more.
A toucan tries to steal our lunch,
We wave it off with a silly punch.

The lizards pose, like starry sprites,
While we wear bowls, our fashion bites.
Grasshoppers sing in a quirky tune,
And we join in like silly cartoon.

Lost in a maze of silly vines,
Playing tag with cheeky pines.
Who knew that laughter could twist and twine,
In this paradise, we feel so divine!

Sipping from coconuts, giddy and loud,
We twirl and spin, feeling so proud.
With smiles that stretch from ear to ear,
Every moment here is filled with cheer.

Mango Moonlight

Under mango trees, we gather round,
The moonlight shimmers, feels so profound.
With sticky fingers and cheeky grins,
We launch into games that nobody wins.

A fruit fight erupts with juicy glee,
Mangoes flying like they're meant to be!
We laugh till we cry, oh what a scene,
Who knew that sweetness could make us mean?

In the warm breeze, we find our tunes,
Singing loudly, beneath the moons.
The stars join in, they giggle too,
Making wishes on the fruit we blew.

As we dance till the morning light,
Wearing mango crowns, oh what a sight!
In this wild, fun-loving island spree,
We embrace the moment, wild and free!

Echoes of an Island Heart

In the shade of a feathery palm,
A crab wears a hat, looking quite calm.
He sips on a drink made of coconut milk,
While seagulls gossip like they're made of silk.

The waves sing songs of fish in a rush,
With laughter that tickles the sandy plush.
A pineapple dance in the breeze, oh so sweet,
As flip-flops go flying from a wobbly seat.

Sunsets paint shades of a frosty pink brew,
While the island's charm makes you feel brand new.
Who needs a map when the fun's in the air?
Just follow the laughter, you're already there.

So raise up your drink and start a grand cheer,
Let's pull out the quirks that we hold so dear.
With smiles so bright, like the sun's deep embrace,
We'll dance with the shadows and giggle with grace.

Eden's Lush Whispers

The parrot is gossiping, squawking away,
About the last party at old Johnny's bay.
He's spreading the secrets of summer's delight,
While the turtles chuckle and take off in flight.

Bananas are dancing, what a funny sight,
With the monkeys all laughing, it's quite a delight.
They swing through the trees, in a wacky parade,
With vines as their floats, they're perfectly made.

Watermelons dive in a splash, such a thrill,
While the fish in their bow ties make quite a skill.
As waves break on shores with a joyful roar,
We'll dance on the sand and always want more.

Let's raise up a toast to the joys that we find,
In this playful Eden that's always so kind.
With laughter echoing through the shimmering night,
We'll surf on a dream, till the morning light.

Island Serenade

A ukulele sings beneath the glowing moon,
As crickets join in, in a whimsical tune.
The stars are the audience, twinkling with glee,
While the palm trees sway as if dancing with me.

A coconut crashes, it rolls down the hill,
While the iguanas giggle, they cannot stay still.
They slip on the sand and tumble with grace,
As the tides come in and they pick up the pace.

Limes are in costumes, all dressed up real bright,
They're ready to party, oh what a sight!
With punch bowls of sunshine, we'll sip and we'll sway,
Underneath the palm fronds where shadows play.

So come join the fun in this island parade,
With friends all around, let's not be afraid.
We'll dance on the beach till the dawn greets our eyes,
With love in the air and laughter that flies.

Sun-Kissed Secrets

Sunshine spills laughter across golden sand,
A crab shows off moves that are simply quite grand.
He's doing the cha-cha with flair and with style,
While tourists take notes, it's sure to beguile.

The smoothies are swirling, a rainbow of cheer,
With flavors so daring that coax out a leer.
Pineapple drummers keep time on the shore,
As beach balls go flying, who could ask for more?

The sunset winks like a cheeky old friend,
Encouraging giggles that never will end.
Let's toast with our jelly-filled donuts today,
For nothing says fun quite like sweetness at play.

So gather around for a tale or a rhyme,
As the moon lifts the veil on this magical time.
With secrets unveiled in the soft, shining light,
We'll keep stashing giggles till the stars fill the night.

Radiant Reflection

In a mirror of waves, I see my face,
Winking at crabs who quicken their pace.
Sun-kissed bananas wear silly hats,
As squirrels dance with acrobatic chats.

Coconuts roll like they're in a race,
While guavas giggle, adding to the grace.
Flip-flops slapping while sand ticks away,
I laugh with the breeze; it's a comical day.

Starfruit Serenade

Starfruit swings high, a fruity delight,
To a tune of laughter under the light.
Papayas gossip with mischievous glee,
While mangoes do cartwheels, wild and free.

A pineapple juggles with lemons galore,
Tumbling and rolling; it's never a bore.
Mirth spills out like juice on the sand,
As oranges giggle with friends hand in hand.

The Scent of Sun

Banana peels slip with a giggly sound,
While sunscreen fights off all the giggles around.
Laughter wafts through the cinnamon air,
Popcorn clouds float; can they dance, if they dare?

Limes play tag with the sun's golden hue,
Splashing in puddles of sweet coconut dew.
Each sip of fruit punch tickles the nose,
As sarcasm ripples wherever it goes.

Celestial Shores

On sandy shores, where the sea takes a peek,
Lemonade waves making fun of the meek.
Sandy toes and silly sea foam hats,
Turtles perform; they're the beach's aristocrats.

Seagulls squawk jokes from their high, lofty flight,
Catching the drift of the salty daylight.
Crispy chips dance on the edge of the tide,
As laughter and sunshine take everyone for a ride.

Vibrant Currents

In a sea of bright cocktails, with umbrellas so spry,
The parrots have parties, oh my! oh my!
Our hats fly away like a kite in the breeze,
While dolphins do flips, saying "Hey, take it easy!"

With flip-flops that squeak on the warm, sun-kissed sand,

We dance with the crabs, feeling fine and quite grand.
A conch shell's our phone, we call for a snack,
"More punch!" we all shout, "and a beach ball to whack!"

The sun's blazing bright, just like our bold shirts,
The coconut's calling with sweet, creamy spurts.
Oh, laughter erupts, like waves on the shore,
Here's to mischief and fun, we're always wanting more!

So here's to the moments we cherish and share,
With colorful drinks and sun-kissed hair.
In our paradise bubble, where joy's taking flight,
We'll party till dark, then dance in the night!

The Call of the Horizon

The horizon is calling, with drinks overflowing,
A piña colada on the way, take it slow, slow!
The sun in our faces, the wind in our hair,
We chase down the seagulls, pretending they care.

Shells scatter 'round, like confetti on sand,
We juggle with starfish; oh, isn't this grand?
The beach volleyball flies like our hopes in the air,
As we dive for the spikes, but a crab takes the dare!

Our beach towels are flying, there's sunscreen afloat,
While we barter for snacks, and take silly notes.
"Not today, little crab! This burger's all mine!"
But he eyes my fries; oh, just wait for the sign!

The sunset's a canvas, with colors that clash,
And we laugh till we cry, with a tipsy old bash.
So here's to this journey, with snacks piled so high,
The horizon's our treasure, and we reach for the sky!

Driftwood Tales

On driftwood we sit, with stories to share,
Like, "Was that really a dolphin or just my strange hair?"
With jellyfish glowsticks lighting the way,
We spill our wild tales while the night roams gray.

The fire's a beacon, of warmth and delight,
As we roast marshmallows that take flight!
With each little bite, a giggle escapes,
As chocolate and chaos create funny shapes.

The breeze carries whispers of tales from afar,
Of treasure maps drawn by our pet, the bizarre.
While shadows do wiggle, believe it or not,
We argue with sandcastles, "You're getting too hot!"

So we'll weave our adventures till the stars all align,
With driftwood as anchors for laughter's design.
Let's embrace every moment, leave worries behind,
In the light of this madness, our joy is defined!

Sublime Shores

At sublime shores where the sun tickles toes,
We chase after seagulls—oh, how it goes!
Our beach games are silly; it's a spectacle grand,
Flip-flops in hand, making castles in sand.

With coconut drinks, we toast to our luck,
As a crab steals our chips—oh, foul little duck!
Yet we laugh as we run, like kids on the spree,
"Come back, little thief! We just want one free!"

The waves roll like laughter, so wild and so free,
And the sun winks at us, a cheeky decree.
With a splash and a giggle, we dive in the blue,
While jellyfish dance to a sea-loving tune.

As day turns to night, with stars taking flight,
We gather our treasures, all merry and bright.
In these sublime moments, our hearts feel the cheer,
With fun as our compass, we know we are here!

Cloudless Daydreams

In a hammock I sway, sipping sweet tea,
The sun tickles my toes, oh joy, so free.
A parrot squawks jokes, he's quite the clown,
While coconuts drop with a comical sound.

Lizards dance by, in tiny flip-flops,
They wiggle and jive, no sign of stops.
Laughing at clouds that float with a grin,
What a fun day in this sun-soaked spin!

Coconut crusted, my worries fly high,
Chasing after dreams as mangoes go by.
The beach sings a song of giggles and cheer,
In this delight, life's worries disappear.

So here's to the laughter, the sunshine today,
All the cloudless daydreams that dance and play.
Life's little moments, with joy we indulge,
Under tropical skies, my spirit's in charge.

Tropic's Gentle Muse

In the shade of the palms, I daydream away,
Where giggles and breezes have all come to play.
A toucan tells tales of a fruit-filled parade,
While pineapples promise a sweet escapade.

With each silly breeze, my hat takes a flight,
Chased by a crab, what a comical sight!
He sidesteps and dances to celebrate flair,
A crab in a hat, oh, who would dare?

The waves laugh along, tickling toes on the shore,
A smoothie in hand, I could not ask for more.
The sun joins the fun, making shadows that prance,
While I join the party in a fruit-punchy dance.

So let's toast to laughter and silly delights,
In this vibrant journey, oh how time flies!
With palms swaying softly, I'll dream till it's night,
Under the moon, keep the giggles in sight.

Under the Mango Tree

Under the mango tree, life's silly brigade,
Dropping ripe laughter, which pops like a cascade.
The peaches roll in, with a slapstick twist,
While banana peels play, you can't help but mist!

A monkey named Larry pulls faces in glee,
Throwing down coconuts—oh, what a spree!
With every wild try, he just misses the mark,
While we all roar with joy in the sun-drenched park.

The lemonade flows like a river of fun,
With sips and sweet slurps, a job well done!
All's merry and bright under citrusy shade,
Laughing with friends, oh, the memories made!

So come join the game, wear a smile or two,
No worries can touch us beneath this sky blue.
Under the mango tree, life's sweet and absurd,
In this fruity escape, let joy be our word!

The Allure of Avocado

Oh, the creamy green fruit, that's quite the tease,
With a pit that rolls round like it's got a disease.
It lures me in close with its buttery charm,
Promising breakfast that's never a harm.

On toast it sings bright, with a sprinkle of zest,
Yet my breakfast dreams always fail the taste test.
It slips and it slides, a comedic delight,
Avocado may win, but I'll put up a fight!

At picnics it rolls, off the plate, what a shame,
While hands play tag with guacamole in game.
The chips tremble lightly, all ready to dive,
As the laughter erupts—oh, what joy is alive!

So here's to the fruit that brings giggles galore,
In salads or spreads, let all voices soar.
With avocado in hand, life's fresh and absurd,
In this playful ballet, let's dance undeterred!

Aromas of the Sea

Fish grilling on the shore, oh what a sight,
Seagulls stealing bites, they've taken flight.
Coconut drinks spill as friends loudly cheer,
Laughter mixes with waves, it's music to hear.

A crab in my lap, I'm not really sure,
If he's just being friendly, or planning a tour.
The scent of sunblock drifts through the air,
While my buddy complains he's lost all his hair.

Tanned shrimp dance on plates, ready to feast,\n"Can I
flip my shrimp?", he yelled, like a beast.
But with every misstep, our joy only grew,
Chasing silly fish dreams, like children anew.

With the beach at our feet and sand in our toes,
Each wave brings more laughter, who knows how it goes?
Sunsets paint the sky in a zany parade,
In this wacky world, we'll never be played.

Enchanted Shores

Waves whisper secrets with a comical croak,
Mermaids giggle while weaving a cloak.
The sun's a banana, oh what a hue,
While I slip on a shell and yell, "Help! It's glue!"

Palms sway to rhythms of a playful breeze,
I tried to dance but fell to my knees.
A lizard on a branch gives me a wink,
As I ponder what color to dye my drink.

Flip-flops are flopping, it's a fashionable mess,
Each step feels like dancing in glittering stress.
A crab throws a party, the guest list is tight,
With shrimp in tuxedos under the moonlight.

Oh, these shores enchant with their goofy delight,
I'll trade all my troubles for a zany kite.
In this land of wonder, where fun takes its flight,
Life's a slapstick comedy, everything feels right.

Midnight in the Tropics

At midnight, the crickets join in the song,
While a pineapple pirate dances along.
The stars are quite tipsy, they twinkle and sway,
As I trip on my towel and tumble away.

In the glow of the moon, I try to impress,
With silly dance moves, it's all just a mess.
My friends are in stitches, they're rolling with glee,
The coconut drinks spill, I'm stuck in a tree.

I spotted a coconut wearing a hat,
And couldn't stop giggling, imagine that!
A firefly flickers, it's guiding my quest,
To find a round fruit, I call it my guest.

The beach at midnight is a whimsical show,
With oddball adventures that only we know.
From dancing with shadows to stories we weave,
In this night of laughter, we'll never leave.

Sweet Nectar of the Night

In the hush of the night, a drink calls my name,
A blend of tropic flavors, but who's to blame?
With straws like giraffes that stretch to the stars,
Each sip is a riddle, like counting to cars.

The fireflies flirt, as if casting a spell,
My friend's doing the hula, it's a sight to tell.
We laugh with the wind, as we sip on delight,
Mixing sweet and salty, like day into night.

An owl joins our party, hooting with flair,
While a starfish critiqued my terrible hair.
A toast to the night, with no reason to fret,
We're all just big kids, and we're not done yet.

So here's to the nectar and funny old dreams,
With fruity concoctions, bursting at the seams.
In this night of enchantment, we dance and we play,
With laughter our compass, we're forever okay.

Coconut Dreams

Under the sun, a drink in hand,
Coconut hats made from the sand.
Monkeys giggle, dancing with glee,
Who knew coconuts could be so free?

Lemonade wishes from a palm tree tall,
Beach balls bouncing, we're having a ball!
Seagulls stealing our snacks with flair,
Oops! There goes my lunch, flying in mid-air!

Sunburnt noses and flip-flop woes,
The more we swim, the more the laughter grows.
Sandy toes and parrot squawks,
Making new friends, with a few funny talks.

At dusk we gather, the fire's bright,
Roasting marshmallows, oh what a sight!
With every bite, the giggles increase,
Coconut dreams, oh what a feast!

Coral Echoes

In the sea, the fish may play,
Coral reefs dance, oh what a display!
Starfish argue over who's the best,
Who knew they had such a zest?

Anemones tickle the curious fins,
As clams gossip about fishy sins.
Seahorses strut in a fancy parade,
With shells for crowns and shells well displayed.

Suddenly a crab, with quite the flair,
Decides to tango right then and there.
With a flip and a flop, he steals the show,
Coral echoes of laughter flow.

At sunset, the sea whispers a tune,
Under the watch of a silvery moon.
With newfound friends, we laugh till we drop,
In this coral nest, we just can't stop!

Waves of Desire

Surfboards waxed, the waves beg to play,
Riding the bubbles, we float all day.
The splash of water, a sudden surprise,
A dolphin jumps up, oh what a rise!

A surfer falls, he's lost in the foam,
His buddies laugh, they call him "Home Alone."
With every wipeout, we cheer and we jeer,
These waves of laughter, perfectly clear!

The beach ball bounces, it's anyone's game,
"Meant for beach fun!" we all loudly exclaim.
Tossing sunscreen as if it's confetti,
Each moment spent, is funny and petty!

As twilight falls, we splash in delight,
Chasing the waves, till they bid us goodnight.
With salty hair and hearts filled with fun,
We dream of the waves, till the next day begun!

Swaying Palms at Dusk

Beneath the palms, we sway in time,
As the day falls, it feels like a rhyme.
Coconuts giggle, the breeze has a chat,
A palm tree whispers, "I'm feeling quite fat!"

The night brings stories from shore to sea,
Of crabs in tuxedos and fish with glee.
We dance on the sand, forgetting our woes,
While the stars above twinkle and pose.

A conga line forms, led by a snail,
Who knew that critters could dance without fail?
With giggles and wiggles, we sway hand in hand,
Under the moonlight, oh isn't life grand?

As shadows stretch long, we gather in cheers,
For the palm tree's wisdom, and all of our peers.
With each sunset, laughter fills the air,
In the sway of the palms, we find we all care!